W9-BGE-222

# LEONARDO
## AND THE
# RENAISSANCE

**Nathaniel Harris**

Illustrated by Martin Salisbury

The Bookwright Press
New York · 1987

# LIFE AND TIMES

Further titles are in preparation

Editor: R.J. Ashley

First published in the
United States in 1987 by
The Bookwright Press
387 Park Avenue South
New York, NY 10016

First published in 1987 by
Wayland (Publishers) Ltd
61 Western Road, Hove
East Sussex BN3 1JD, England

ISBN 0–531–18137–5

Library of Congress Catalog Card Number: 86–73003
Phototypeset by DP Press, Sevenoaks, Kent
Printed in Italy by G. Canale & C.S.p.A. Turin

# Contents

# 1 THE MYSTERIOUS GENIUS

## The young Leonardo

Renaissance Italy was an amazing place, producing a host of great rulers, writers, soldiers, thinkers and artists. But Leonardo da Vinci is probably the most famous of all these Renaissance men and women. Although he had many gifts, he is chiefly remembered as an artist, and every year many thousands of visitors go to look at the *Mona Lisa* and other Leonardo paintings in museums and galleries.

Leonardo was born on April 14, 1452, in a village

Adoration of the Magi, by *Leonardo, which hangs in the Uffizi Gallery in Florence.*

near the little Italian town of Vinci; his full name, Leonardo da Vinci, simply means "Leonardo of Vinci." The important city of Florence was not far away, and when Leonardo's father realized how talented his young son was, he apprenticed him to a leading Florentine artist named Verrocchio. At about this time, Leonardo made a careful study of lizards, snakes and bats, and then painted an imaginary monster on a shield. It was so lifelike that when his father saw it he almost turned and ran. When he was about twenty, Leonardo painted an angel in the corner of a picture by his master, Verrocchio. It was so beautiful that Verrocchio is said to have sworn to give up painting because he could not match his pupil.

*Leonardo working in Verrochio's studio where he studied the art of painting and other crafts.*

# The "universal man"

**Above** *Lodovico (called the Moor) gave Leonardo a position at the court of Milan.*

**Below** *Leonardo's* The Last Supper.

In sixteenth-century Italy, people with a wide range of talents were admired far more than specialists. Leonardo was an outstanding example of this kind of "universal man." He made his reputation as an artist in Florence. Then in 1482 the Florentine government sent him on a mission to Milan — not as a painter but as an expert musician. Leonardo liked Milan so much that he asked the city's ruler, Lodovico Il Moro (Lodovico the Moor), to employ him. In his letter to Lodovico, Leonardo mentioned his artistic gifts, but wrote much more about his abilities as a military engineer and his skills in designing fortifications and deadly weapons of war.

Leonardo was given a position at the court of Milan, and he then took on all sorts of new jobs. He organized and probably wrote plays and pageants, decorated rooms and even designed cathedrals. But he became famous throughout Italy for two works of art: a large

model of a horse and rider, and a wall-painting, *The Last Supper*. Leonardo stayed in Milan until 1499, when it was captured by French troops. Tragically, the soldiers celebrated their victory by using Leonardo's horse and rider for target-practice, and it was completely destroyed.

*Leonardo at work on his masterpiece*, The Last Supper, *painted on the wall of a monastery in Milan.*

# The later years

Once he had left Milan, Leonardo found it hard to settle down. He wandered about Italy, staying in Mantua, Venice and Florence. He was employed by the ruthless general Cesare Borgia, to design and oversee the construction of fortifications in central Italy, and at one time thought of going to work for the Sultan of Turkey.

While he was in Florence, Leonardo painted the *Mona Lisa*. This is still the most famous portrait in the world, showing a mysterious, smiling woman against a romantic background of rocks. Leonardo is said to

*The* Mona Lisa, *which now hangs in the Louvre, in Paris.*

have entertained Mona Lisa herself with groups of musicians and jesters, just to make sure she would keep smiling until he finished the painting.

In 1513 Leonardo's wanderings eventually led him to Rome, which was becoming a great artistic center. But Pope Leo X much preferred the work of younger artists such as Raphael and Michelangelo, and less and less attention was paid to Leonardo. Then in 1516 he was invited to settle in France, where he had an enthusiastic admirer in the new young king, Francis I. Leonardo went, taking the *Mona Lisa* with him. The King gave him a splendid house not far from the royal palace at Amboise. He often consulted Leonardo and honored him greatly at his court until the artist's death on May 2, 1519.

**Below** *Leonardo paints the* Mona Lisa *while musicians keep his model entertained.*

**Above** *A self-portrait of Leonardo in old age.*

# Leonardo's notebooks

Leonardo's personality remains something of a mystery. He labored continuously yet completed only a handful of paintings. He left many works unfinished, and delivered others months or even years late. His great engineering projects were never even begun. And his experiments sometimes had disastrous results, as when a faulty experimental technique failed to stop *The Last Supper* from decaying.

This may mean that Leonardo was a perfectionist, never satisfied with what he had done and yet impatient to move on to something new. We know that his mind teemed with ideas, because his notebooks have survived — thousands of pages of drawings, records, experiments, observations and plans. The words are written backward and right-to-left, as in mirror writing. Perhaps they were intended to be secret; or perhaps Leonardo, like some other left-handed people, found it comfortable to write that way.

There are certainly no personal secrets in the notebooks that could shed more light on Leonardo's personality. They show that his greatest interest was in how and why things worked. He dissected bodies and made superb anatomical drawings. He studied mathematics, medicine, the movement of water, and many other subjects. He drew fantastic machines from imagination — machines we now know as submarines, tanks and helicopters. In his all-embracing curiosity and achievement, Leonardo was a true representative of the Renaissance spirit.

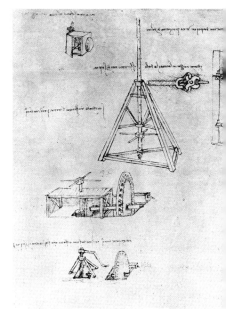

**Above** *Some of Leonardo's drawings. These include a lantern with lens, a drill and a power-driven wheel.*

**Left** *Leonardo was fascinated by how and why things worked. His mind teemed with ideas: mathematical problems, medicine, flying machines, underwater machines – everything interested him.*

# 2 WHAT WAS THE RENAISSANCE?

## A new outlook

*A young Florentine nobleman, painted by the Renaissance artist Botticelli.*

The Renaissance is the name given to a new way of life that first appeared in Italy. It lasted from about the fourteenth to the sixteenth century, and during this period there was a great change in the way people thought about themselves and the world around them.

More than anything else, the Renaissance was based on the belief that human life was supremely interesting and valuable, and that "man can do all things." This self-confidence owed a great deal to the wealth of Italy, a land full of big bustling cities, industries and trades. Here there were wonderful new opportunities for adventurers, artists, scholars, architects and musicians. Splendid buildings and beautiful works of art were created. Men and women tried to develop all their talents to the full — that was why they had such an admiration for "universal men" like Leonardo. Trying to understand the past and improve themselves in the present, they opened up new subjects of study. And, thanks to the recent German invention of printing, their new ideas and new knowledge spread more widely and quickly than ever before.

"Renaissance" means "rebirth." Strangely enough, Italians did not think of themselves as doing something new: they believed they were reviving the glories of ancient Greece and Rome, whose history provided models of the kind of lives they themselves wanted to lead. But although they often imitated the ancients, Renaissance Italians nevertheless found themselves creating a new society.

**Below** *Renaissance men and women liked to relive past glories and yet were interested in improving their own lives and developing their talents to the full.*

# The great cities

During the Renaissance, Italy was divided into many states of varying sizes. Most of these had grown up around a city that had gained territory by conquering its neighbors. So even when they were quite large, such states were named after the ruling city. When we talk about "Florence," for example, we sometimes mean the city, and sometimes the city-state stretching across the region of Tuscany. And Leonardo is always called a Florentine because the town of Vinci belonged to Florence.

Mantua, Urbino and other small cities made valuable contributions to the Renaissance. But the most important Renaissance centers were the four

*The city of Florence in Tuscany was the major cultural and artistic center of the Renaissance.*

most populous and powerful cities. These were Florence, Venice, Milan and Rome.

The republic of Florence produced far more great writers, artists, financiers and men of action than any other city-state. These included the poet Dante, the sculptor Michelangelo and Leonardo himself. Venice, also a republic, was the greatest Italian naval and trading power in Italy. It had been built on the islands of a lagoon, and had canals instead of streets. Milan was a powerful dukedom. Rome was slightly different, since the pope, who ruled over most of central Italy, had his headquarters, the Vatican, in the city. All of these centers were transformed during the Renaissance, as proud rulers and citizens equipped their cities with magnificent public buildings, churches and palaces.

# The wealth of Italy

The Renaissance was made possible by Italy's wealth. Elsewhere in Europe, most people lived and worked on the land. Money was used only by a few and the practice of art and learning was mainly confined to the Church or royal courts. But in Italy there were also merchants, bankers, traders, lawyers and many other city people who were willing and able to buy books, build fine houses and employ artists and musicians. They paid for Renaissance culture, which was largely shaped by their tastes.

Part of Italy's prosperity came from manufacturing. Florence was famous for woolen goods, and later for silks, which were exported all over Europe. The iron industry of Milan produced armaments, and the shipbuilding industries of Genoa and Venice were vital, since international trade was the lifeblood of the Italian city-states.

Italy was ideally placed by geography. In the eastern Mediterranean, Italian merchants could buy the spices and luxury goods that Europeans wanted. They then transported them through Italy to central Europe, or shipped them through the Straits of Gibraltar to northern Europe.

Through their international trade, Italians developed the financial skills they needed for their far-flung dealings: banking, credit, checks and insurance. The most famous bankers were the Medici family, who became rulers of Florence and great patrons of Renaissance culture.

*Foreign trade was vital to the Italian city-state and the ports were busy shipping goods all over Europe.*

# Renaissance ideals

**Above** *Lorenzo de' Medici who ruled Florence from 1469–92, was a distinguished scholar and patron of arts.*

Renaissance men and women did not aim just to excel, but to achieve all-around excellence. They believed that men should, for example, be capable of fighting well, and also of talking intelligently and dancing gracefully; that the physical and mental sides of life should be in harmony. This was an ideal held by the ancient Greeks almost two thousand years earlier, and is one of the reasons why they were admired so much by the men and women of the Renaissance.

Like the Greek and Roman heroes, Renaissance men and women wanted to make the best of their lives, to be successful and, if possible, famous. To achieve these goals, they were prepared to study and learn, and others were prepared to teach. The Renaissance was the first great age of "do-it-yourself" books. Machiavelli's *The Prince* told its readers how to seize and keep power. Della Casa's *Galateo* taught them table manners. And Castiglione's *The Courtier* advised them on how to succeed at court — even how to tell good jokes!

Leonardo was not the only "universal man" who achieved excellence in many areas. Much earlier, Leon Battista Alberti shone as an architect, soldier, horseman, musician, writer and painter — and boasted that, with both feet together, he could jump over a man's shoulder!

**Left and right** *Men and women of the Renaissance were prepared to study in order to enhance their lives. They were eager to do things for themselves and the age produced people talented in many fields.*

19

# 3 RENAISSANCE CULTURE

## Art and artists

The paintings, sculptures and buildings of the Italian Renaissance were probably the greatest achievements of the period. People realized this at the time and began to feel that great artists could no longer be looked on as mere craftsmen. The modern idea of the artist as a special kind of person has its start in the Renaissance.

In painting, there was a slow but radical change. Most pictures painted during the Middle Ages — the period before the Renaissance — were of religious subjects. The painter did not try to copy life, his aim was to stir up religious emotions. Renaissance artists continued to paint religious scenes, but in a new way, emphasizing their human quality — and that meant painting Jesus and other figures realistically, as convincing human beings in a real landscape. The great Florentine painter Giotto painted like this as early as 1300, and generations of Renaissance artists followed along the path he had laid out. Increasingly, too, people were painted as individuals rather than types, and the Renaissance was the first great age of portraiture since Antiquity (ancient Greece and Rome). Renaissance artists gloried in human beauty, whether clothed or naked. Inspired by Greek and Roman statues, sculptors such as Donatello created the first nude figures in many hundreds of years.

In architecture, too, Greek and Roman models inspired daring new works, including the huge dome of Florence's cathedral and a wealth of splendid palaces and country houses.

*Renaissance men and women greatly admired the ideals and the heroes of ancient Greece and Rome.*

**Above** The Virgin of the Rose *painted by Raphael, one of the great artists of the Renaissance.*

**Below** *The great dome of Florence's cathedral was one of the many architectural glories of the Renaissance.*

# Writers and musicians

The Renaissance admiration for the Greeks and Romans showed itself most clearly in literature. Every educated person tried to write in pure Latin (Greek was less used) in the style of the ancients, and many lost and forgotten writings by Greek and Roman authors were tracked down and published. The experts in this field were the scholars, writers and teachers known as humanists — a name that pinpoints the human values that the Renaissance treasured in Greco-Roman culture. But in their own writings, the humanists tended to imitate the ancients too closely. They were excellent scholars, but they rarely showed originality.

However, despite the prestige of Latin, many

*Detail from a representation of Dante amid scenes from his Divine Comedy.*

**Below** *Early Italian opera was based on the mythology of ancient Greece and Rome.*

Italians began to write with increasing skill in their native language. One such was Dante, the Florentine poet whose *Divine Comedy* is considered the greatest long poem written in Italian. Machiavelli, Castiglione and others wrote their books in Italian prose, and the Renaissance emphasis on human individuality led to the writing of some excellent biographies and autobiographies.

In music, the Italians' most original contribution was made around 1600, when the Renaissance was almost over. A group of Florentines decided to create Italian versions of ancient Greek tragedies, which, they believed, contained long passages of singing. They were wrong in their belief, but their mistaken efforts gave rise to a new form of musical drama, the opera.

# Science and medicine

The people of the Renaissance tended to believe that the ancients had solved all the most important problems. Ancient Greek writers, such as Galen on medicine and Aristotle on science, were regarded as infallible authorities. People were discouraged from looking and experimenting for themselves, and this was the reason for the slowness of scientific progress.

Leonardo da Vinci was an outstanding example of a man who insisted on finding out for himself. He dissected many creatures and made superb anatomical drawings that might have revolutionized medicine. But he never published his work, which lay forgotten for centuries. Twenty-four years after Leonardo's death, a book by Andreas Vesalius, who taught at Padua, was to be the foundation of the scientific study of anatomy.

The greatest Italian Renaissance scientist was Galileo Galilei. He made an improved version of a new Dutch invention, the telescope, and used it to look into space. He saw the surface of the moon, the stars making up the Milky Way, and the satellites of Jupiter — observations that upset all the fixed notions people held about the universe. Later he took up a theory put forward by the Polish astronomer Copernicus, that the earth moved around the sun instead of vice versa. The Church authorities forced him to take back his opinion, but of course he was later proved right.

**Below** *Galileo demonstrating his revolutionary theories about the nature of the universe.*

# The Renaissance Church

**Above** *Cesare Borgia once employed Leonardo to design military fortifications. He was probably the most ruthless of the infamous Borgia family.*

Renaissance Italians were intensely interested in the world around them, and studied it much more carefully than people had done during the Middle Ages. But, like their predecessors, they were also deeply religious, and the Catholic Church strongly influenced their lives. The leading figures of the Renaissance included many churchmen, and one pope, Pius II, was an outstanding humanist writer.

The pope was the spiritual head of the entire Catholic Church. But he was also an earthly ruler who held power over Rome and central Italy. The trouble with this situation was that many popes found themselves acting more like tough politicians than religious leaders. One Renaissance pope, Julius II, even put on armor and marched at the head of his army!

Renaissance popes spent money lavishly to beautify Rome. Apart from its ancient monuments, the wonders of the present-day city are mainly their creation — including St. Peter's, the largest church in all Christendom.

Despite such brilliant achievements, Renaissance popes tended to be less admirable as Christian leaders. The most notorious of them was Alexander VI, who bribed his way to the papal throne. He also fathered several children (which Catholic priests are forbidden to do) and favored his own family, the Borgias. Alexander's son, Cesare Borgia, who employed Leonardo for a time, was a particularly ruthless general.

**Right** *Pope Alexander VI outside St. Peter's in Rome.*

# 4 LIFE IN RENAISSANCE ITALY

## Work and play

**Calcio** *a form of football that the Italians loved to play.*

Most men and women in Renaissance Italy worked on the land. They tilled the soil or herded animals, just as their ancestors had always done.

But there were many more townspeople than in previous times. A great number of city-dwellers were craftsmen and belonged to guilds, which also had a long history. Guild members included masters (men who ran their own workshops), journeymen (fully trained workmen), and apprentices (boys learning the craft). Painters had their own Guild of St. Luke's, and Leonardo had to train in Verrocchio's workshop before he was allowed to become a full member.

There were plenty of items for sale in the bigger cities, available in the single-room shops, which were open to the street during the day and shuttered at night. All the shops and workshops connected with a particular craft or trade were usually concentrated in the same quarter of the town.

Renaissance Italians liked sports and games, such as hunting, running, wrestling and chess. They were also great gamblers, and enjoyed playing games with cards and dice. Two popular events in Florence were the Palio, a horserace right across the city, and the Calcio, a sort of rough-and-tumble football match in which a good many of the fifty players were likely to break their bones.

**Left** *A busy street scene in an Italian city.*

# Festivals and pageants

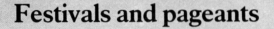

Renaissance people loved colorful public occasions. These gave the rich people a chance to show off, and kept the poor amused with free entertainments. At pageants, those who could afford it often wore fancy dress, perhaps appearing as orientals or as ancient Romans. Another popular entertainment was the tournament, where knights and horses were decked out in highly decorated armor and embroidered cloth.

Plays drew large audiences to the churches and public squares where they were performed. However, courtiers tended to prefer masques, which were less dramatic but more lavish and extravagant than plays.

*The Italian cities each celebrated certain festivals – many of them with torchlit processions.*

While he worked in Milan, Leonardo is known to have created a *Masque of Paradise* for Lodovico Sforza (Il Moro), devising ingenious working models and a revolving stage.

All the Italian cities had their own popular festivals. In Florence, the feast of St. John the Baptist, the city's patron saint, was the high point of the year. The citizens of Florence celebrated the festival with long, candlelit processions and a series of mobile shows and models, wheeled around in carts. On Ascension Day in Venice, a unique ceremony was performed to mark the city's special relationship with the sea. The head of the Venetian government, the Doge, was rowed out of the city in the huge state barge, the *Bucentaur*, followed by a fleet of gilded gondolas. Then he solemnly "married" the sea by flinging a wedding ring into the water!

# Renaissance women

Women were primarily wives, mothers and home-makers in Renaissance Italy. Poor women worked about the house and in the fields, and also helped their husbands in their workshops. The wives of wealthy merchants had servants and nurses to help them, but their lives, too, were quite narrow and restricted.

Hardly anyone married for love. A poor man needed a strong, willing helper. A middle-class man thought first of the cash settlement (dowry) offered by the bride's parents; girls without dowries had little chance of finding husbands. Princes and nobles married to increase their territories or ally themselves with powerful families.

**Below** *Women of the upper class enjoyed a life of ease with time to follow interesting pursuits.*

Once wedded, a girl was supposed to obey her husband in everything. She probably did, since most brides were about thirteen years old, whereas men married quite late in life.

However, the wealth of Renaissance Italy did give large numbers of upper-class women time and leisure that could be put to good use. Some held court in splendor, surrounded by admiring poets and artists. A few, such as Michelangelo's friend Vittoria Colonna, wrote poetry and were able to influence religious life. Occasionally, as in the case of Isabella d'Este, a woman was able to run a state efficiently, acting on behalf of her absent husband or small son.

**Above and below** *The lives of poor women were hard and many worked all day in the fields.*

# Childhood and youth

*Upper-class boys spent long hours studying.*

Childhood was very brief in Renaissance Italy. Boys and girls were petted and played with only until they were about six or seven. Then they were expected to dress and behave like adults. Of course they still got into mischief, but they were likely to be severely punished when they did so.

Poor children worked from an early age, helping their parents in workshops and fields, or being hired out as servants. The sons of better-off people were expected to study hard with private tutors or in school. Girls rarely went to school, though the luckier ones might receive a very good education at home. Latin was the basis of all education, but some children had mastered several languages by the age of ten. Learning was mostly memorizing and texts were drilled in with the help of frequent beatings. However, there were a few humanists who held the revolutionary belief that learning should be made interesting and should be taught with kindness!

For the children of the nobility, education was not just a matter of book-learning. Boys were taught to handle weapons, while girls learned elegant embroidery. And both boys and girls were drilled in social skills such as good manners, graceful movement and dancing.

*A woodcut showing children, dressed in their normal, adult clothes, playing a game of skittles or ninepins.*

# Fashion and manners

*This detail from a painting by Gozzoli, shows Lorenzo de' Medici (the Magnificent) dressed in the beautiful and extravagant clothing of Renaissance nobles.*

Equally colorful clothing was worn by both men and women. The basic male outfit consisted of a shirt, waist-high hose (stockings) somewhat like modern tights, and a close-fitting doublet similar to a jacket. Women wore high-waisted dresses with neat, often low-cut bodices.

From time to time governments tried to stop their citizens from dressing extravagantly, and passed laws laying down what each social class should wear. But they had little success in enforcing them. People who could afford to, dressed elaborately, adorning their costumes with furs, embroidery and jewels. Fashions came and went with bewildering speed, and some were quite fantastic: costumes that were parti-colored, for example, with different-colored legs, or slashed, with slits in the fabric through which the lining was pulled. Women used cosmetics freely and, since it was fashionable to be blonde, they dyed or sun-bleached their hair.

The modern code of simple, natural good manners appeared first in textbooks written by Renaissance Italians. As a people they were much cleaner and more conscious of hygiene than other Europeans, and this led them to give up eating with their fingers. One of Italy's important gifts to civilization was something that is now in general use — the fork!

**Opposite** *Both men and women dressed in elaborate fashions that changed frequently.*

# Fighting for pay

During the Middle Ages, the citizens of northern Italian towns had fought for their independence against the Holy Roman Emperor, who was based in Germany. In Renaissance times, as they grew wealthy, the rulers of city-states often preferred to hire mercenaries — men who were paid to fight and who had no other reason for loyalty to their employers. These mercenaries are often known by their Italian name, *condottieri*.

Loyal and successful mercenary commanders could expect to be honored and rewarded by their employers. Two of them, Gattamelata in Padua and Bartolomeo Colleoni, became the subjects of equestrian (man-on-a-horse) statues by great Renaissance sculptors. A third, less loyal, but more spectacularly successful, was Francesco Sforza, who seized the throne of Milan and founded a dynasty.

Wars between Italians were rarely bloodthirsty. The *condottieri* who were employed by the various cities had no strong reasons for killing one another. They preferred to fight battles by careful maneuvering rather than mass slaughter. This system worked well enough when Italian armies met each other, but it collapsed when Italy was invaded by the larger and more energetic forces of foreign powers. When this happened, the Italian states proved unable to act together for very long, and from 1494 on, Italy suffered greatly as the country became a battleground, fought over by French, German and Spanish armies.

*A sixteenth-century* arquebusier, *(a soldier with a portable gun).*

**Left** *Mounted mercenaries who fought for pay. If they pleased their employer they might be rewarded with honors; if they did not, their fate might well be execution.*

# Brief glory

The early sixteenth century in Italy is often described as the High Renaissance — the brief period in which the Renaissance reached a glorious climax. This is a little unfair to fourteenth and fifteenth century Italy, but it is certainly true that three supreme artists were at work after 1500: Leonardo da Vinci; the sculptor and painter Michelangelo; and Raphael, a brilliant young painter from Urbino.

During this period Rome became the greatest artistic center in Italy. Here Michelangelo painted the huge ceiling of the Sistine Chapel, and Raphael created other masterpieces for the pope's palace, the Vatican.

Then the glory began to fade. In 1519, at the age of sixty-seven, Leonardo died; Raphael's death followed in 1520. In 1527, after a quarrel between the Emperor Charles V and Pope Clement VII, the Emperor's German mercenaries captured the city of Rome and brutally sacked it.

The sack of Rome is sometimes called the end of the Renaissance. But of course, great movements do not end so suddenly. Italy continued to produce great men. These included the scientist Galileo, the composer Monteverdi, and the painter Titian, who came from Venice.

However, as we have seen, Italy was now suffering from invading armies of foreign powers and the country's prosperity was affected through the opening up of new sea-routes beyond the Mediterranean. As a result, the great flowering of art and culture in Italy's city-states began to fade. But by this time the Renaissance was spreading outside Italy.

La Pieta, *the magnificent sculpture by Michelangelo of the Virgin Mary holding the body of Jesus Christ, now in the Vatican.*

**Opposite** *The sack of Rome.*

# 5 THE SPREAD OF THE RENAISSANCE

Portrait of a Scholar *by Hans Holbein; he was a German painter much influenced by the Italian Renaissance.*

Foreigners who came to Italy — often as invaders — envied its great monuments and splendid culture. One invading king, Louis XII of France, even wanted to cut Leonardo's *Last Supper* out of the wall it was painted on, and take it back to his native land! More usefully, early sixteenth-century rulers such as Francis I of France and Henry VIII of England began to import Italian artists into their countries to design and decorate their palaces, paint their portraits and carve their statues. It became fashionable for artists and scholars from northern European countries to visit Italy and for noblemen to tour the country. The German painters Dürer and Holbein, and the Dutch humanist Erasmus, were among the great sixteenth-century Renaissance figures. Renaissance ideas, styles and manners continued to spread even though Renaissance Italy had begun to decline.

But Europeans did not just copy the Italians. Each country took what it wanted from the Renaissance without abandoning its own traditions. New influences began to take effect, especially the Protestant Reformation, launched in Germany by Martin Luther against the worldly popes and other weaknesses of the Catholic Church. And writers such as Shakespeare and the French essayist, Montaigne, although quite different from Renaissance humanists, could not have achieved what they did without the great trailblazers of the Italian Renaissance.

**Right** *In northern Europe, scholars, writers and painters took up the concepts and ideals of the Italian Renaissance.*

Erasmus

Luther

Shakespeare

Dürer

Holbein

43

# Table of dates

| | |
|---|---|
| **c.1300–50** | Early Renaissance. Dante writes *The Divine Comedy*. Giotto produces the first Renaissance paintings. |
| **1434** | Cosimo de' Medici takes over the government of Florence. |
| **1450** | Francesco Sforza becomes Duke of Milan. |
| **1452** | Birth of Leonardo da Vinci. |
| **1475** | Birth of Michelangelo. |
| **1483** | Leonardo settles in Milan. Birth of Raphael. |
| **1492** | Rodrigo Borgia becomes Pope Alexander VI. |
| **1494** | Charles VIII of France invades Italy. Beginning of Italian Wars. |
| **1498** | Leonardo finishes *The Last Supper*. |
| **1502–03** | Leonardo works for Cesare Borgia. |
| **1503** | Guiliano della Rovere becomes Pope Julius II. |
| **c.1504** | Leonardo paints *Mona Lisa*. |
| **1506** | Building of St. Peter's Church in Rome, begins. |
| **1508–12** | Michelangelo paints the ceiling of Sistine Chapel. |
| **1516** | Leonardo settles in France. |
| **1519** | Death of Leonardo. |
| **1527** | Sack of Rome. |
| **1543** | Vesalius publishes *The Fabric of the Human Body*. |
| **1550** | Vasari's *Lives of the Most Eminent Painters, Sculptors and Architects* published, reflecting the fact that artists are no longer thought of as just craftsmen. |
| **1564** | Death of Michelangelo. Birth of Shakespeare. Birth of Galileo. |
| **1609** | Galileo uses his new telescope to study the stars and planets. |
| **1633** | The Inquisition forces Galileo to take back his assertion that the earth goes around the sun. |

# Glossary

**Anatomy** The study of how bodies (plant and animal) are constructed.

**Bodice** Close-fitting upper part of a woman's dress, above the waistline.

**Calcio** A 25-a-side game played in Florence in Renaissance times. It was like a no-holds-barred form of rugby football.

*Condottiere* (*plural condottieri*) Italian word for a commander or soldier who fights for pay, not through love of his country or because he is forced to.

**Dissect** to cut up as part of the study of anatomy (see above).

**Doge** The elected head of the Venetian state.

**Doublet** Close-fitting, jacket-like man's garment.

**Dynasty** Line of rulers belonging to the same family.

**Equestrian** Having to do with horseback-riding.

**Guild** Association of people in the same trade, including employers, workers and apprentices.

**Humanists** Scholars and writers, experts in ancient Greek and Latin literature.

**Hygiene** The science of cleanliness and the maintenance of health.

**Masque** A performance rather like a play, but with less action and drama. The emphasis on poetry, music and colorful scenes made the masque a popular form of court entertainment.

**Mercenary** Soldier who fights for pay (see *condottiere* above).

**Middle Ages** Period of European history, lasting from approximately A.D. 900 to 1500. The Middle Ages ended earlier — about A.D. 1300 — In Italy, where the Renaissance began much sooner than anywhere else.

**Notorious** Famous for evil or immoral deeds.

**Palio** A popular horserace across the city of Florence.

**Sack** The violent looting of a city or other place, usually accompanied by killings and other atrocities, widespread destruction, etc.

**Slashing** Sixteenth-century fashion in clothing. Many cuts were made in a material; then the lining or fabric beneath was pulled through, making a pattern of different-colored fabrics.

**Vatican** The huge residence of the popes, in Rome.

**Picture acknowledgments**

Bridgeman Art Library 4, 8, 21 (top), 36, 42; Mary Evans Picture Library 23, 39; Mansell Collection 6 (top and bottom) 22, 26; Ann Ronan Picture Library 18 (bottom), 29, 33, 35; Topham Picture Library 18 (top); Zefa 21 (bottom), 40; Wayland Picture Library 9, 11, 12, 24, 25

# Further information

## Places to visit

*Art galleries and museums* Most of Leonardo's paintings now hang in art galleries. The *Mona Lisa* and other works are in the Louvre Museum, Paris. The National Gallery in London has *The Virgin of the Rocks* and a famous cartoon (full-size preliminary drawing) for *The Virgin and Child with St. Anne and the infant St. John*. There are other, somewhat less important paintings by Leonardo in Florence, Munich, Cracow, Leningrad and Washington, D.C.

The Renaissance produced so many wonderful works of art that most of the great national collections of Europe and the United States include at least some. The museums and galleries of Italy are outstanding. Among the most famous are the Uffizi Gallery, the Bargello Museum and the Pitti Palace in Florence; The Accademia in Venice; the Brera in Milan; and the Vatican in Rome.

*Buildings and cities* As well as their galleries and museums, the great Italian cities contain abundant treasures from the Renaissance period. Florence, for example, is full of splendid palaces and churches. Rome has the great church of St. Peter's and the Sistine Chapel (part of the Vatican). The remains of Leonardo's *Last Supper* are still to be seen on a wall of the monastery of Santa Maria delle Grazie in Milan. Many Italian churches are interesting in their own right and also contain masterpieces of painting and sculpture; most of Giotto's greatest pictures, for example, were executed for the Arena Chapel in Padua. Donatello's equestrian statue of Gattamelata is also in Padua, whereas Verrocchio's Colleoni monument stands in Venice. Urbino, Mantua, Orvieto and many other towns are also well worth visiting.

## Books

Davidson, Marshall B. *A History of Art from Twenty-Five Thousand B.C. to the Present*. Random House, 1985.

Konigsburg, E.L. *The Second Mrs. Giaconda*. Atheneum, 1975.

Middleton, Haydn. *Everyday Life in the Sixteenth Century*. Silver Burdett, Co., 1983.

Powell, Anton. *Renaissance Italy*. Franklin Watts, 1980.

Sabin, Francene. *Renaissance*. Troll Associates, 1985.

Tynan, D.M. *Leonardo Da Vinci*. Cambridge University Press, 1977.

Wallace, Robert. *The World of Leonardo*. Silver Burdett, Co., 1966.

# INDEX